God at Work
part II

GW00692033

David Sheppard
Bishop of Liverpool

James Allcock
Director of Gas Supplies at British Gas

Robert Innes (Editor)
Theological Researcher and Part-time Tutor,
St John's College, Durham

GROVE BOOKS LIMITED
BRAMCOTE NOTTINGHAM NG9 3DS

Contents

Editorial Preface

This booklet is the third of a series of three booklets published by Grove in 1994 on the subject of 'Work'. The series arises largely out of the 1993 Anglican Evangelical Assembly (AEA) which took work as its main theme.

The first booklet, published in March 1994, was Grove Pastoral booklet 57: *A Christian Understanding of Daily Work* by the Rt Rev Graham Dow. Its aim is to help Christian people consider the place of their daily work in the purposes of God, and can be used as a study course. The second booklet (*God at Work part I*), published in July 1994 in the Grove Ethics Series, began with an exposition by Dr John Goldingay of God at work in Genesis 1. I then looked (in Chs 2-6 of the booklet) at Lutheran and post-Enlightenment ideas about work, and explored how the Spirit of God might be at work in the culture of the modern corporation.

This booklet contains three articles. The first, 'God's Concern for the World of Work' is taken from the lecture given at AEA by the Bishop of Liverpool, the Rt Rev David Sheppard. David Sheppard has had many years of ministry in urban, industrialised situations. This article contains some of his reflections on the reality of working life in such contexts and his thoughts on relating the world of church to the world of work. The article reflects the bishop's special concern for the poor and unemployed. The second article, 'The Experience of Work', is taken from the AEA lecture by James Allcock, Director of Gas Supplies at British Gas (writing in a personal capacity). In it Mr Allcock explores the contradictions between the ideal of work, a noble calling to care for the earth, and the reality of work in a fallen world. The article also tells us how a senior industrialist thinks the church can best equip its members to serve God more effectively in the working world. In the third article, 'The Power of the Consumer', I seek to argue that improvements to our working lives will only come about if they are matched by ethically informed spending by the consumer.

We hope that the three booklets between them will provide a lively and wide-ranging contribution to a subject that has until recently been largely neglected in church circles.

Robert Innes

The Cover Picture is by Greg Forster
Copyright David Sheppard, James Allcock and Robert Innes 1995
First Impression January 1995
ISSN 0951-2667
ISBN 1 85174 284 0

God's Concern for the World of Work —
David Sheppard

1

Bridging the Gap Between
the World of Church and the World of Work

The Gap Between Church and Work

I begin in the world of Church:

- It is the last part of an overnight parish visit, and I have been invited to an evening with the PCC together with other leaders of organisations in this parish. We have agreed four themes for a wide-ranging discussion. One theme is the growth of adult members of this church; I try to draw them on how their Christian faith influences them in their daily work. One person engages eagerly with the subject, other eyes go glassy. It is clearly not a subject that is on the parish agenda.
- 'Tell me what your faith means to you this week', a lay worker asked a senior executive of ICI. 'Well', he said, 'On Saturday my wife is running a stall in the parish sale. I shall get the car out and take the produce she's been preparing down to the Church Hall'.
- A senior police officer, a regular member of his parish church in Liverpool, never discusses any matter relating to his work when he is in church.
- As Bishop of Woolwich I was told by commuters who lived in the parishes near the Surrey/Sussex border that they heaved a sigh of relief when their train went through a particular tunnel. They had left London behind.

These experiences are typical of the divorce which so often takes place between the world of church and the world of work. Yet the most worrying issues in many of those lives were to do with work. God the Creator and Sustainer blesses the creation of wealth and the sustaining fabric of society; He cares about good relationships in the Company and the damage that redundancy will mean for individuals. These people believe that, but they have come to assume that no help is to be found within the fellowship of the church. Why should this be?

One reason might be that they think clergy will inevitably be soft about some of the decisions they believe have to be taken: 'Bishop, you won't agree with this, but...' and a manager tells me about a painful decision. When we discuss the matter we realise that serious ethical issues are involved, and that there is no obvious right answer. He is glad to have the opportunity of talking it through in a Christian context.

Perhaps many worshippers simply don't connect daily work matters with their church life. As a result many Christians feel very much alone when it comes to some quite complex matters. That feeling of being left on their own may be a major reason why Christian insights are not expressed in board room, shop stewards meeting or town hall.

Bridging the Gap

If we truly believed that a Christian's first calling is to do his or her daily work to the glory of God, we would expect to affirm that work within our worshipping life, would we not? Yet many worshippers do not even know what their brothers and sisters in Christ, who sit next to them in the choir, do all day.

Some parishes have a map of the world with photographs of link missionaries connected by a line with the place where they serve. Why not a similar map of the city or the county with photos of members of the congregation and a note of what they do? Why not a regular place in the intercessions where office workers, managers, teachers or farmers were named in turn with particular matters they had mentioned for thanksgiving or prayer? In a large congregation perhaps these cameos could be shared in house groups; it would also be highly appropriate when ecumenical groups meet.

Archbishop Worlock and I went to put the case for maintaining the Liverpool factory to the chairman of an international company during the decade when Merseyside lost 10,000 jobs net per year. We were waiting downstairs. The receptionist said to us, 'I know why you've come. I'm a Christian. I'll be praying for you when you're with the chairman.' As we went up in the lift Archbishop Derek said, 'There's a lot of it about'. It is a great encouragement to Christians to know that a lot of Christian presence and support is about.

The church has resources which could help and interpret, but we often ignore them. Whilst Industrial Mission will never cover the ground of every place of work, it holds together a network of Christians who acknowledge that they need help to think Christianly about their working lives. We do not set apart industrial chaplains to take over the witness from lay people; rather, it so that it so that they may do their living and their theological reflection in the context of work, or in some cases in the context of no work along with unemployed people. Parishes could invite them as resource persons when issues at work are being discussed or celebrated. I fear that the reason they are not invited is often the defensiveness of the vicar. He thinks he should be omnicompetent, or he fears some of his ablest members being brought under influences he cannot control. Perhaps it is the same fears which prevent vicars commending their commuter members to city centre or town centre churches where they might well be encouraged to meet and think with their peers.

Let me do a little 'bridging' now myself. During a recent reading week I was studying 1 Corinthians at the start of each day. I reflected on how Paul sought to cast the light of the gospel on the events of his day. The climax of the letter is chapter 15—the extended proclamation of the resurrection of Jesus Christ and of those in Christ. Here in the resurrection is the vindication of Christ's way of working and living, of the way of the cross in which Paul glories: no theology of success here! In the letter daily matters are seen in the light of the resurrection and of eternity. Gifts of prophecy, tongues and knowledge will pass away. Three things last for ever: faith, hope and love.

Paul also goes to work with an expectation which did not come true. In chapter 7 he said, 'The time we live in will not last long'. The parousia was coming very soon and so he could write, 'I think the best way for a man to live in a time of stress like the present is this—to remain as he is...married men should be as if they had no wives; mourners should be as if they had nothing to grieve them; the joyful as if they did not rejoice; those who buy should be as if they possessed nothing; and those who use the world's wealth as if they did not have full use of it'. We now know that the Master is a long time coming; our end time may or may not be soon. But the promise of resurrection and eternity sheds its light on the married, the mourners, the joyful, those who buy and those who use the world's wealth.

Let me take up the last two of these. In the business city there are real issues about short term and long term policies. The light of the resurrection emphasises those things which last. In the future God will make new heavens and a new earth which will be the home of justice. The more seriously we take that promise the more unbearable are the contradictions to that promise with which we are confronted in everyday life.

1 Corinthians 15 makes it clear that the gospel is a gospel of grace. In the climactic chapter 15, Paul tells his own story: 'By the grace of God, I am what I am'—who once persecuted the Church. In his labours he had outdone them all, 'not I indeed, but the grace of God working with me'. At the beginning of the letter it is all about gift; there is no place left for human pride for it is by God's act. God chose by the folly of the gospel to save those who have faith.

When he comes to look at particular issues—sexual behaviour and food offered to idols—he does not appeal to laws or apostolic pronouncements from the Council of Jerusalem. The light of the gospel of resurrection and of grace is cast upon sexual behaviour in chapter 6: the body is special for it is to be raised. You were bought at a price. Your are the temple of the Holy Spirit. So honour God in your body. Concerning food offered to idols: knowledge puffs up but love builds up—and love lasts for ever. There is one God, the Father, one Lord, one body. So there needs to be care for the weaker brother and no giving of offence to Jew, Greek or the Church of God. Yet also in chapter 10 there is a remarkable statement of reclaimed land. You may eat anything sold on the meat market without raising questions of conscience, 'for the earth is the Lord's and all that is in it'. He has reclaimed the land for his use. Commercial and industrial enterprises which have behaved like idols towards their employees and their competitors can be reclaimed for his use, becoming more modest, more accountable.

2
The Daily Journey and the Calling to Work

The Protestant Work Ethic in Today's World

If the church intervenes in political or economic debate, we are likely to be told sharply that we should stick to the spiritual. It is worth commenting, however, that 'laissez faire' is itself a classic political stance. By saying nothing and doing nothing we are indeed being political, for we are then supporting the status quo. In the Middle Ages the church condemned usury. When ways were found of saying that money of itself was not wrong the way was opened up for one of the most influential ways in which the church has ever intervened, namely the formation of the Protestant work ethic. At the heart of this ethic lies the idea of the 'calling'. In the Middle Ages Christians had understood God's calling generally to be to the religious life in some form. Now the powerful motivation of God's calling was brought to bear on daily work.

I want now to look again at what I said about the Protestant work ethic in the Dimbleby Lecture that I delivered in 1984. I spoke of the creative power of this ethic for the development of the environment, for promoting innovation and for creating wealth. I expounded on three features of the ethic which are easily forgotten. Firstly, a true sense of the work ethic has something transcendent about it. The calling comes from beyond our world, from God who cares for the whole. And the work ethic responding to his call should also have something transcendent about it. For the effect of what we do in our daily work ripples out far beyond merely achieving tasks and earning money. It affects our colleagues, customers, shareholders, the neighbouring community, the unemployed, rival manufacturers and nations. Believing that there is one who calls us gives us a sense of proportion and of accountability.

It stops us seeing only our achievement and reminds us of God's grace that equips us. If we lose the transcendent dimension, there will only be arid, utilitarian concepts of work.

Secondly, I said that a true sense of the work ethic has something fraternal about it. In response to the *Faith in the City* report published the year after my Dimbleby Lecture, the 'New Right' appealed to the illustration of the marching column. They said that the faster the front ranks progressed the further forward the back ranks would be drawn. But what that illustration ignored altogether was the reality of relative poverty. Relative poverty hurts when, for example, poor people look through their only window on the world, the television. High pressure advertising tells them that the normal life of British people needs the products they see. They and their children then feel shut out from the normal life around them.

Thirdly, and linked to the second point, a true sense of the work ethic carries with it a strong notion of what is just. Freedom for the strong to press forward at the head of the marching column may be in conflict with the justice for the poor which prophets like Amos, Isaiah, Micah, Jeremiah and Ezekiel spoke about. Now it is argued that the free market is the most efficient way to run the world's economy. I agree that competition will very often make for efficiency. But whilst the absence of government intervention looks efficient to the strong, a widening gap between governors and governed makes for dangerous alienation and anger which could smash all our proud growth.

I delivered my Dimbleby lecture at a time when a Militant-led council in Liverpool was leading our city to the brink of confrontation with the government in Westminster. I said that I hoped the arguments of people like me would be would be listened to and that the city council would pull back from the brink. I went on, 'But I fear greatly that Comfortable Britain will then heave a great sigh of relief and forget all about Liverpool'. In recent years a typical enquiry has been, 'Things are better in Liverpool, aren't they?' Well, it's a Tale of Two Cities. There is Enterprise City, helped by the government's City Challenge; the leadership of the city council is pragmatic and co-operative. Enterprise City is holding its own modestly well, although without increasing employment. Alongside Enterprise City is Hurt City, large areas which have endured unemployment for two or more generations. The number of business births in Merseyside in the 1980s just about matched the percentage increase nationally. But the number of business deaths was substantially higher. Merseyside is moving very close to joining Northern Ireland in being the only regions in the UK to qualify for European Community 'Category One' status. This status is given, we hope with substantial supporting grants, to a region with average incomes of 75% or less of the EC average.

So let me take a look at the 'daily journey' and the 'calling' for three different groups: those who have the privilege of regular work; those who bear the burden of management; those who are unemployed.

For Those Who have the Privilege of Regular Work

The three features of the Protestant work ethic that I singled out in my Dimbleby lecture seem very contemporary to me for the privileged regular worker:

1. We should be aware of something transcendent about our calling, carrying out our work with thankfulness and accountability to God, the Caller. We are to be aware of something transcendent about the effect of our work on others.

2. A fraternal attitude to work means, amongst other things, welcoming equal opportunities programmes. Workers at every level have the power to either promote or damage prospects for black people, women and the handicapped.

3. A strong sense of justice will question what is being done for those who are left out of the good opportunities. it is one of the least lovely features of our public life that those who claim that they have pulled themselves up by their own bootstraps often speak harshly and judgementally of those who are poor today. They sometimes suggest that anyone who worked hard enough could pull themselves up as they have done. One or two points could be made in the face of such comments: 'Tell me about your mother'; 'Does the grace of God only come to the deserving?'; 'If you have self-confidence you should thank God every day for it.'

For Those Who Bear the Burden of Management...

Sometimes those in management feel the church is always critical and fails to understand. I hope that we genuinely want to enter into the pressures they feel. Because business policies affect the whole life of the community we shall also want to argue with them sometimes. Moreover, to argue with someone is to take them seriously.

I am very aware of some of the burdens of management and I salute those who are willing to bear them. The reality of a manager's life has to do with efficiency, marketing, competition, with staff training, good communications, with public relations. The pressures which managers talk about to our Liverpool Industrial Mission chaplains and parish clergy include, 'a constant stream of reorganisations from above', 'industrial pollution', 'short term profits'. But a good work ethic tries also to move beyond these pressures to the wider effects of business life on the community.

...Responsibilities to the Community

Unfortunately some businessmen dismiss any questioning of values. They say that they are in business to stay in business. Industrial Mission chaplains talk to me of a changed atmosphere in many places of work from twenty years ago; in an age of deregulation rocking the boat is not lightly tolerated. Indeed, in the process of sweeping away the clutter, the presence of an Industrial Mission chaplain may simply be regarded as part of the clutter. I even read of a Christian banker saying, 'Don't let your business judgement be infected by Christian ideals.' Yet I believe there are many in management who value the presence of those who have the courage to hold up the mirror to them so that they can see what they are doing to each other. They welcome being reminded of some values which are easily forgotten. A Christian insight insists that life is not to be lived in separate compartments. God is the God of the whole earth. It is certainly his will that the earth be developed and wealth be created. The light of the gospel is to shine both on how wealth is created and on how it is distributed.

Archbishop Worlock and I chair the Michaelmas Group, a group of senior businessmen in Liverpool. We have been meeting monthly over breakfast for more than eight years now. What brings us together is a common concern to help in any way we can with the regeneration of Merseyside. I think each of the group would hold that they serve their own company better for sharing in our attempt to look at the whole picture.

One member of the Michaelmas Group moved to London on becoming a senior director in his company. I introduced him to the Dean of St Paul's, through whom he joined a group in the business City of London. They were meeting to see how they could respond as businessmen to Faith in the City. He told me that the group fell into two. One part felt their whole aim was met in trying to see how they might distribute profits more effectively for those at a disadvantage. The others thought this was part of the aim, but also thought that the methods by which wealth is produced affects Urban Priority Areas.

Indeed, many businessmen recognise that, although they do not live in Urban Priority Areas, they are gatekeepers of opportunity for these areas. They may, for example, open—or close—gates of employment to UPA people by monitoring recruitment policies in their company. They may, or may not, support investment in these areas by their decisions on insurance and banking facilities for UPA projects. For example, I am repeatedly told that company policies may rule out projects in areas where insurance is seen to be more risky.

...Countering Discrimination

Some groups feel that the gates to employment are unfairly closed against them. Black and Asian young people continue to be at a relative disadvantage in seeking jobs, with Pakistani, Bangladeshi and Afro-Caribbean young people having the highest unemployment rates. Young black people in Liverpool still have very low expectations of finding jobs. Mass unemployment is generations deep. A survey in 1939 of 200 black heads-of-household in Liverpool showed 74% unemployed. More recent surveys show rates remaining at the 50% level. Some years ago a Liverpool black girl asked me when I met a fifth form, 'Why don't black people get jobs in the stores or in buses or on the trains? They do in London. I know, because I've lived there.' Another youngster said to his youth leader, who was encouraging him to go after a job, 'You don't only expect us to be twice as good as whites, you want us to be pioneers and to go where no black people have gone before'. Despite this disillusionment amongst black young people, some firms I know have determined not to give up. Persistent monitoring of application forms and the supply of good training facilities mean that in one firm I know black people are now gradually finding senior posts.

Some years ago I was one of a small number of church leaders who spent twenty four hours with a group of black young people from New Cross, South London. It was an uncomfortable time. They insisted that we should understand their strong feelings about being shut out from good opportunities in training for jobs, in education, in representation in the media, and in having a stake in the way decisions are made. The young man who chaired the consultation said very firmly, 'It seems to some of us, looking up from below, that there is a network of people who make decisions. We should like to be part of that network.'

Black and Asian young people often and with good reason expect to be stereotyped, as do girls. Other groups can be stereotyped too, for example those with particular postal codes. A colleague who has recently moved from Newcastle told me that church-based community workers in districts like Meadowell were encouraging young people not to include their post code on applications. They said that young people from Meadowell Estate might as well forget applying for a training place. That may not be the fact, but, as with black young people and those who work with them in the community, that is what they feel. That feeling often becomes as real as any facts. I am frequently reminded that when Nathanael heard where Jesus came from his comment was, 'Can anything good come from Nazareth?' That is the question many employers ask when they read the postal code on applications. Perhaps they wouldn't have given that young carpenter an interview either.

For Those Who Are Unemployed

Many want to shift all the blame onto young people themselves; they are dismissed as layabouts who do not want to work. That is said less often now that unemployment is touching families who never expected it before. One clergy son is helped by a member of the congregation to write letters on her computer. She told me that they have written over 300 letters seeking jobs without success. That is in a Lancashire parish, part of Comfortable Britain, where many church members have been inclined to say that anyone who wanted to find work could do so.

A priority in helping people to help themselves in areas of high unemployment should be second chance learning. I am talking especially about colleges of further education. Liverpool Community College has 30,000 students, many of them otherwise unemployed. It offers a series of planks in the bridge which can develop God-given abilities. In a way the subject of the first course matters very little. It must simply engage someone's interest and begin within the culture and experience from which the student comes. More often than anyone would dream such courses can lead on to Access courses and they in turn to higher education.

A very talented woman who teaches in further education told me of how fulfilling she found her work. At the same time she compared the resources available to her with those given to her husband teaching business studies at the University. She did not begrudge him the magnificent equipment at his disposal, but it sharpened her sense of the low priority that we give to those who are trying to catch up.

Employers would do well to visit and make some investment in colleges of Further Education. Where unemployment is high, the disincentive to work hard for those of school age is very heavy. The experience of many is that the penny drops some years later, with the discovery that someone possesses abilities that are worth developing. The penny drops for all sorts of reasons and at very different ages. I have met colleges of further education where confidence is growing, where adults who had seen no point in working at school are now firmly set on courses which will equip them with highly significant skills. Take the example of one young woman describing a year's course in Liverpool:

'Before I started the course I was a bored, unemployed and disillusioned single parent, with no job prospects and no ideas on how to pull myself and my son out of the rut that had developed around me. It was my mother who introduced me to the course, herself a student the previous year. On the course I gained confidence to make new friends, a lot of whom were in the same position as myself. I learned how to study. I also learned that I had a thirst for good books. I had not read a book for at least three years. One of the most important things that I learned from

Second Chance was a craving to learn further and the courage to carry it out. I am studying a Maths course for teaching and a GCSE English language course. I hope to start a B.Ed. course.'

Or take the case of a young man who left school with no qualifications at all, believing that he would never get over the problems that he had with English. Through adult basic education he now realises that it is not as difficult to overcome these problems as he had thought. He went on to study on an Access course, hoping eventually to gain professional employment. And, quite as significantly, he realised that he could now be a role model for his children, showing them the doors that learning can open and helping them realise that an 'ordinary person' in his area can 'make it'.

When I had completed ten years in Liverpool, people in the Diocese were kind enough to say that they would like to establish a Tenth Anniversary Trust for whatever cause I would like. I said I wanted the Trust to make grants in the field of second chance learning and to help those who are unemployed become more employable. Although we have done quite well, with the Trust having passed £70,000, we can only make modest grants. But every quarter we receive perhaps thirty applications. My point is that many of those I hear about are desperately poor. They tell me that £50 to help with fares makes all the difference in the world. When they left school they were mostly low achievers. Now, for one reason or another, the penny has dropped and they are absolutely determined to go on that educational journey, to make the most of themselves and, wherever it is possible, to find employment.

You will have picked up some of my enthusiasm for second chance learning! It follows that I believe as a nation we should give much higher priority to further education. It follows, too, that employers need to open their minds to the talent that they could discover from such routes. That means that they should give proper weight to National Vocational Qualifications (NVQs) as marking the genuinely transferable skills that second chance learners have developed.

The Experience of Work—James Allcock[1]

1

Some Biblical Insights on the Place of Work in Human Life

The first we hear of work in the Bible is not in connection with man but God. Two fundamental activities are described—work and rest—and they lead to one outcome, which is satisfaction. 'On the seventh day, God finished his work which he had done and he rested...and God saw everything that he had made, and it was good' (Gen. 1:31). After the initial period of creative activity two further steps were taken to make the world productive. The world needed rain and it needed a gardener. In response to these needs God brought up mist to water the earth and created a gardener. Our job from the start has been to work, and the commission given to man is essentially the same before and after the fall: 'the Lord God took the man and put him in the garden of Eden to till it and to keep it (Gen. 2:15)....Therefore the Lord God sent him forth from the garden of Eden to till the ground from which he was taken (Gen. 3:23)'.

Now Dorothy Sayers, in her 1942 *Essay on Work* said,

'Work is not primarily a thing one does to live; but the thing one lives to do. It is, or should be, the full expression of the worker's faculties, the thing in which he finds spiritual, mental and bodily satisfaction and the medium in which he offers himself to God. We should no longer think of work as something which we hasten to get through in order to enjoy our leisure: we should look on our leisure as the period of changed rhythm that refreshes us for the delightful purpose of getting on with our work.'

Certainly this is more biblical than the classical view: both Plato and Aristotle thought of work as an evil necessity from which man should seek to escape. But it has more than a whiff of the opposite mistake, the divinisation of work. Thomas Carlisle, for example, said, '*laborare est orare*'. He went so far as to say that work is the latest gospel in this world. The biblical teaching is not quite the same as what Dorothy Sayers has in mind. Man looks up and down, up towards God and down towards the ground. Looking up reminds him of the Creator and looking down reminds him of his origin and destiny as fallen man. In this sense the old Catholic saying, '*ora et labora*' is nearer the mark. Man has two occupations not one. We are neither gods nor beasts; we

1 The views expressed in this article are those of the author and cannot in any way be taken to be the views of British Gas Plc.

are human beings. We bear the image of God but are rooted in the earth.

From the Genesis account it is clear that our task is as gardener or steward of what God has made, and I would emphasise this. We have heard a great deal during the 1980s about the creation of wealth. For me this smacks of the arrogance of modern man. I am not sure that scripture supports the idea that we are the creators of anything. Procreation is probably the nearest we get. It is the givenness of everything that comes over in the first and second creation accounts: 'Behold I have given you every plant yielding seed...and I have given you every green plant for food...You may freely eat of every tree in the garden except...' (Genesis 1.29, 2.16). It is good for modern men and women to remember that, despite our technological expertise, everything we have is a gift of God. Our own ingenuity and the things we apply to it are given to us by him.

Work is fundamental to understanding who we are as human beings. Therefore a man is held in contempt if he will not work—'if a man will not work neither shall he eat' (2 Thess. 3.10)—and is held to be sorely deprived and frustrated if he cannot work through infirmity or lack of opportunity. Similar reasons apply in both cases: in the first instance he denies one of his own *raisons d'etre*; in the second case he is unable to fulfil this basic human purpose even though he recognises it.

2

In Defence of the Protestant Work Ethic

From the little reading I have done it is clear that the Protestant work ethic is under fire. Reviewing Michael Moynagh's book *Making Unemployment Work*, Francis Pym writes, 'In time it will be recognised that finding a new moral framework for employment to replace the increasingly outdated work ethic will, in its own way, be as important as economic and political attempts to solve the problem. And John Stott, writing in an All Soul's Paper of 1979 said, 'The so-called Protestant work ethic has tended not only to encourage industry, but also to despise those who are losers in the struggle for survival, because they are either shirkers or because they are weak'. There is, I believe, in these statements a criticism of the work ethic which is undeserved.

According to Luther the way of living acceptably to God was not to surpass worldly morality in monastic asceticism, but through the fulfilment of the obligations imposed upon the individual by his position in the world.

That was his calling. I am defending this view. The calling of all men is to work, and this meant originally to till the ground and to keep the garden. This is not outdated. The Reformers never said that a man's intrinsic worth was measured by his paid employment. Undoubtedly the intention was that man should be profoundly fulfilled in his being by the work that he does, and this work is what we would call secular today.

By an odd irony, a view reminiscent of the Catholic monastic position has been influential in evangelical circles in my own lifetime. There is no doubt that when I was a student there was put before us a hierarchy of callings: the church; then medicine; then teaching; then law; and, for the morally bankrupt and feeble-minded, industrial and commercial life! To the extent that this view has been influential in evangelical circles, I think it has been costly. Nonetheless, the single-minded insistence that young evangelical men, and now presumably women, should go in for full-time ministry has revolutionised the influence of the evangelicals in the Anglican Church in my generation. Maybe our new task is to equip young men and women to do the same thing in the City, in industry and in public life as they have done in the Church of England. If so we will need to:

- Offer them grounds for believing that the devotion of their best energies and the best years of their lives to this task is intrinsically worthwhile in a biblical perspective.
- Successfully disabuse them of the idea that these occupations are necessarily 'dodgy' from an ethical point of view.
- Create institutions corresponding to the theological colleges we have for ordinands in which to train them theologically for their secular tasks.

That is why I have tried to assert, with the Reformers, that our daily work is our calling as men and women and that the old monastic distinction between the *vocatio spiritualis* and the *vocatio externa* must not be smuggled back into evangelical thinking in terms of a hierarchy of acceptable and worthwhile occupations.

I also want to make a plea for Christian education. The education many of us received from our university and college Christian Unions was rightly directed largely to the devotional development of our relationship with Christ, with evangelisation and with the enjoyment of fellowship. It did not, and will not, equip young Christian leaders to address the issues they will face in politics, in the Civil Service, in the City and in industry and commerce. Educating young people to deal with these situations is a specialised task. Likewise, I do not think that it is the job of parish priests to minister directly to interest groups within their congregations. I want my vicar to unfold for me the meaning of the faith, to re-open my eyes to the glory of the Lord and to call me back to obedience and trust. I do not want to hear his amateur comments about what I should and should not be doing in my business.

Two of the specialist Christian educational resources with which I am personally associated are:

- *Christian Impact*. If I were in a position to do it, I would insist that between university and first appointment all Christian Union members, and certainly those embarking on a career in public or commercial life, should attend their long course 'The Christian in the Modern World' or at least attend their shorter Summer School. I would urge clergy to acquaint themselves with the services available from Christian Impact and recommend these courses to young people in their congregations.
- *The Ridley Hall Foundation*. This foundation aims to provide high quality courses which help participants to integrate their business life with the Christian faith more effectively; to provide high quality written material relating Christian theology and ethics to the business world; and to help those training for ordination to be better equipped for ministry to and with business people.

These institutions cater largely for those with university education who can be expected to reach positions of some seniority. Most young people leaving school and going into industry will, of course, pass their time in positions of considerable subordination and in increasingly unattractive cultural environments. It is urgently necessary to develop corresponding means of support for them.

3

Work As it is Experienced

Dorothy Sayers commented in her *Essay on Work*, 'His [the worker's] satisfaction comes, in godlike ways, from looking upon what he has made and finding it very good.' But only a small proportion of the working population would recognise that as a description of the way they spend their time. An academic, a craftsman, even a bishop might recognise this description of work, but would a docker, a coal miner, a shop worker or any kind of junior office worker? For most of these, life, real life, begins on Friday evening when, with wage packet, they meet their friends in Pizza Hut or pub, and it ends late on Sunday evening, or even early on Monday morning, as the shadow of the working week returns. Ask them, Dorothy, if they live to work or work to live!

There are, to my mind, four principal reasons for this disparity between

16

the essential enjoyment of work and the common experience of it, which I shall now discuss in turn.

The Consequences of the Fall

I am simply not competent to interpret the meaning of the curse as it has worked itself out in our experience of work, but it is clear that there was a change in the relationship between man and the ground that he was set to till. After the fall there is alienation in work; there is unremitting toil; there is profitless work; there are occupational hazards; there are destructive diseases of livestock and crops. Maybe the other issues I am about to discuss are expressions of the curse. We cannot wholly escape the consequences, but as Christians we look forward to the ending of creation's long, drawn out 'groan'. The creation will one day be set free from its bondage to decay and obtain the glorious liberty of the church of God.

The Division of Labour

The division of labour has cost has dearly. Very few of us actually till the ground. The psychological involvement and the theological exercise—to till the ground from which we came—are lost to most of us. The primary industries of fishing, agriculture and mining, employ not more than 1.5% of the gainfully employed. Most of us have lost our daily touch with creation. There is no mud on our boots, no wind in our hair or coal dust in our eyes. The division of labour, and to some extent the substitution of capital for labour, has cost more in terms of quality of life than we realise. The division of labour was famously advocated in *The Wealth of Nations*. You remember the pin makers:

> 'If ten men had wrought separately and independently and without any of them having been educated in this peculiar business, they certainly could not have made twenty, perhaps not one pin, in a day; not a four thousand eight hundredth part of what they are at present capable of performing in consequence of a proper division and combination of their different operations.'[2]

We have made ourselves unbelievably rich in material things since the eighteenth century, first by this division of labour which so improves labour productivity, and then by the substitution of capital for labour. This is the choice we have made, but it is a choice that comes with a psychological price-tag. None of Adam Smith's ten men ever made a pin again. One draws the wire, one cuts it, one makes the head and one fixes the two together. We all know this. I myself work in a hermetically sealed office and in climate controlled cars and restaurants. Sometimes when I get home I have no idea whether

---

2   From Adam Smith *The Wealth of Nations* Vol 1.

the day has been cold or hot, wet or sunny. As a result I can become pathetically sentimental over the feeblest DIY woodwork completed with much huffing and puffing in the garden shed. The fulfilment of directly created work, however simple and botched up, leads to overwhelming joy. I do not see any way back in terms of the management of our economic lives, but I think that he is a misguided man who so conducts his work as to leave no room for direct physical expression of himself, whether in wood or metal work, music or sculpture. We all need, I am convinced, to till the ground from whence we came, in one way or another, if we are to have a balanced and unfrustrated life.

For most ordinary people the matter is much more serious than that. Need I spell out, particularly to those who come from industrial areas, what most people (those who have jobs) spend their time doing and how soul-destroying it can be?

Management Attitudes

The third reason for the disparity between the ideal of enjoyment and fulfilment in work and the actual experience of work for many people is down to management. You cannot claim to be in charge and not accept responsibility for the atmosphere and relationships within which people work. The aim should be that the time we spend in our 'production mode', which is, after all, the better part of our waking lives, should be as enjoyable—yes, even as fun—as our 'consumption and leisure mode'. Some theories of management deliberately prevent this from happening. I have tried in my working life to give people who work for me space to be themselves and to create an atmosphere of co-operation and comradeship rather than fear. With what success, it is for others to judge.

The Impact of Some Aspects of the Market Economy

I pointed out earlier that the original biblical distinction was between work and rest, and that the period of rest was given quality by the contemplation of what had been achieved. In the market economy the distinction is different. There is the time we spend earning and the time we spend spending. This is not the same thing at all. For example, when I was young, I climbed up mountains in the summer and skied down them in the winter. No-one paid me to do either, but it was much harder work than that for which I was paid in the rest of the year. The point must be emphasised for it is the heart of the matter.

The biblical categories of work and rest are replaced by the new concepts of employment and unemployment because, in a market economy, value is expressed in money terms. Work that is valuable, real work, work worth doing, is paid for. Our value system is a money value system. Society's contempt is now directed at those who won't take paid employment and our pity is extended to those who can't find paid employment.

There are two possible responses to this change from biblical to market-orientated categories:

1. There are those who say our value system must be changed so that people's morale can be maintained even though they are not gainfully employed. They must be persuaded that they can be using their energies in useful service, and that they can be stewarding the earth in a biblical sense even though no-one gives them a weekly pay packet for their work. This I call the radical response.

2. There are those who despair of changing our value system in that sense and insist that the object of policy must be to provide paid employment for all who want it, because the frustration and despair of unemployment cannot be relieved in any other way. This is the conventional view.

It seems to me that the Christian view could never be that all values can be expressed in money terms. However, that only sharpens the problem of our appropriate response. If we are going to intervene in public policy our proposals have to be capable of implementation. I must ask the radicals, who are sure that they have righteousness on their side, if they understand the scale of what they are proposing to achieve. For they will not succeed in re-educating us in the concept of value in the context of work unless the whole value structure of our society is shifted.

I support the conventional view for two reasons:

a) I do not believe that we would succeed in persuading the unemployed that cultivating bits of waste ground, or tidying up derelict areas, or clearing swamps, or flattening coal tips is satisfying work. They know that, in a market economy, society would put a value on this work if society thought it valuable. In short they would be employed by a firm to do it. Representing the 'radical' position, Donald Hay, writing in *Economics Today*, suggests that, 'From the biblical point of view [unpaid work] is just as much work as forms of employment, and is accorded the same "status" of requiring the exercise of responsible stewardship. Just because someone is unemployed does not mean that they are not working or that they should not be expected to use their time productively.' He goes on, 'How this might be organised is another question.' It is indeed! It is a question to which he does not return, neither does he tell us how he would distinguish between 'productive' and 'unproductive' work unless measured by the wage it attracts.

b) If we were to shift our energies into teaching people that there is a fully satisfying life without paid work, we would take the political pressure of government to provide reasonably full employment.

4
The Task of Creating Jobs

Thus I do not think our discussion of work can avoid the more general macro-economic arguments about the creation of jobs. Here, I think we must acknowledge at the outset that the problem is not one-dimensional. It is important to say this. Christians who live and work close to the evidence of long-term unemployment understandably become passionate about it, but it is not the only issue. After all, there was no measurable unemployment in the Soviet Union, but the cost of this arrangement was manifestly too high in other respects. We do not have the luxury of a single policy objective—the eradication of unemployment. Again we must acknowledge that, ever since the 1944 White Paper, governments of all complexions have been committed to the search for full employment with stable prices, but that it has proved an elusive goal. Our first aim must therefore be to try to develop a clear understanding of the technical reasons for unemployment in our economic system, so that we are then in a reasonable position to argue about the ethical implications of different policies for doing something about it. My own analysis of this problem highlights two factors as follows.

The Problem of Combating Inflation

There is an endemic tendency for democratic regimes to be inflationary. The democratic process involves promising what cannot be achieved. This produces an unrelenting pressure on the big spending departments—Defence, Social Security, Health and Education—to spend more real wealth than is available. Inflation is caused by seeking to accommodate spending programmes ahead of the growth of real income. Escalating inflation has eventually to be squeezed from the economy with high interest rates and reductions in spending programmes. During these forced periods of re-adjustment unemployment rises far above its 'natural level'.

The Problem of Establishing an Appropriate Clearing Wage

Theoretically there could be wage levels at which all the unemployed would be absorbed into employment. If these wage levels are very low, it is because the potential productivity of this labour is very low. There are two possible reasons for low labour productivity. Either there has been inadequate capital investment, or the skill levels of these people in relation to the market place are low. Essentially, what is happening is that the wage rate at which the labour market would be 'cleared', i.e. at which there would be no long term unemployment, is regarded, as a matter of political judgement, as being unacceptably low. Therefore a certain part of the labour supply remains unemployed and its standard of living is subsidised by those in employment.

Tackling the first problem is a matter of keeping government spending under proper control. The second problem, which I wish to pursue a little, relates, in large part, to improving the educational levels of the workforce. This latter applies, broadly, to two quite different cases: school leavers and the middle aged.

Too many of our school leavers lack marketable skills. I believe that the debate about monitoring and raising education standards through national tests is important for the future of our industrial economy. The objections of the teaching profession to classroom testing are at two levels. Philosophically, some teachers do not believe that teaching is about imparting knowledge to those who would otherwise be ignorant. To them, the idea of trying to assess how much has been successfully imparted is ridiculous. On the other hand, many of the rest who do not have such objections are merely resisting the measurement of their professional effectiveness.

This battle must be won. The sixteen year-olds lounging around Toxteth and Newcastle and Brixton and St Paul's, Bristol, have been let down by my generation and the ravages of 1960s educational philosophy. We shall not escape the consequences. We earn our living in a global market. There is, in the Far East, in Japan, China, Indonesia, Malaysia and so on, a huge economic dynamo and a labour force that is highly intelligent, industrious and increasingly well educated. However compassionate we may feel for the youths of our city streets, there is no hiding place in our society from these international realities.

I would not like you to think that this view goes unchallenged by radical writers. For example, Alan Lipetz, in his *Towards a New Economic Order*, says, 'It is criminal…to promise young people that more education and training will get them a job. For any given level of education and training, the more a person has, the better the chance of a job; but if the level rises, this does not mean there are more jobs available. It simply means there will be better educated unemployed people.' I disagree with Lipetz. Better education means more jobs because education raises the general level of labour productivity.

On a more modest level, much more money must be spent on retraining the middle aged. Typically these people have more wisdom and self-discipline than the young, but less energy and flexibility. Governments should be encouraged to co-ordinate the timing of retraining initiatives with large structural changes in the economy. Indeed the problem of re-training the middle-aged highlights our need for a new attitude to education in general. In an environment where the skills required are changing so fast, education must now be less about the imparting of specific skills and more about learning how to learn. We have to accept that learning and relearning will be a continuous process occurring throughout our working lives.

And finally…

Dear rectors and vicars and priests-in-charge, do not shrink with an overwhelming sense of inadequacy when you see me, a businessman, in the pew. I do not want you to solve my problems from the pulpit. There was written inside the pulpit of the Old Chapel of St Paul's, Portman Square, so that only the preacher could see it as he climbed the steps, the words, 'Sir, we would see Jesus'. Do that for me on Sunday morning. Show me him in all his glory and I will return to my stewardship with new strength. As Christians we have a noble calling and awesome responsibility. We have a dual stewardship: stewards of his world and stewards of the mysteries of Christ.

The Power of the Consumer—Robert Innes

It is not possible properly to address the problem of work in modern society—the supply side of the economy—without some very brief remarks about patterns of spending and purchasing—the demand side of the economy. It is sometimes said in industry that, 'the customer is king'. British manufacturing companies are typically driven by their marketing and sales divisions. We rightly talk of spending *power*. National policy under Conservative governments from 1979 onwards has been to extend this power to sectors such as education and health. Good and healthy patterns of work will be hard to sustain if the weight of consumer buying power acts against them. The right use of this increasing power is a matter of values: it is essentially a theological and moral issue.

How and in what quantities individuals purchase goods is, in a modern capitalist society, a matter of freedom of choice. But these choices are not morally neutral. In my article in the Grove Ethics Booklet *God at Work part I* (Chs. 2-6) I suggested that 'good work' involves the supply of products with respect for wide social, ecological and temporal horizons. Each purchase stimulates a demand for a product that has been produced in a particular way, and this way may or may not have taken these horizons seriously. Sometimes the moral implications of a purchasing act are obvious. Take, for instance, the well-publicised effect of the demand for hardwood furniture on the tropical rain forests. Or consider the decision to employ an immigrant woman as a cleaner at a very low rate of pay in the knowledge that she desperately needs a job and has no bargaining power. In other cases, and more typically, we are shielded from the effects of purchases by mass markets and intermediaries. We rarely need to think about the conditions under which the goods we buy are produced nor do we encounter those who produce them. But this does not, however, empty the consumer's free choice of moral content.

According to Ricardo's notorious 'Iron Law of Wages', wages naturally fall to the level needed to keep that number of labourers alive at subsistence level which is necessary to meet the demand for their products. For example, the low price of coffee could be said to be related to the 'natural' population of coffee plantation workers. Whether or not we agree that this fixes the 'natural' price, it certainly does not fix a just price. The just price for coffee, or any other commodity, is one that accords genuine value to the labour supplied in producing it. Buying cheap goods is stealing someone's labour.

The Victorian social critic John Ruskin wisely observed that the real value of a nation's wealth depends on the moral sign attached to it. Our accumulated possessions may indicate hard work, scientific progress and efficient modes of production. On the other hand, they may reflect unjust trading systems whereby the rewards of labour in a weaker country are transferred to a stronger country. In the first case we have solid and real wealth. In the second case, really and objectively before God, our wealth is valueless.

Until quite recently it would have been thought hopelessly idealistic to influence consumer spending by appeal to ethical principles. Market economics assumed that customers behaved 'rationally' by maximising the personal 'utility' of their goods for the minimum expenditure. However, the ecological movement has placed at least one set of moral criteria firmly on the table. The necessary correlate of a proper theology of work is the acknowledgement that spending power, like other kinds of power, is to be used to empower others, to bring life and to build genuine wealth. And, as Ruskin once observed, wise consumption is actually a far more difficult art that wise production.

We should try to recover attitudes to goods and services which value them primarily as 'divine blessings' (Calvin's phrase) rather than just as artefacts to which our spending power entitles us. To purchase wisely is both to be blessed by God and also to bless the producer. 'Wisdom' in purchasing involves discrimination as to those production processes that we feel it is appropriate so to 'bless'.

One thing that can help us all to value our goods more is to gain a better understanding of how things are actually produced and manufactured. We are all irritated when there is a power cut. But how many of us appreciate the huge complexity of the modern power station, or stop to think about the astonishing level of co-ordination of labour and skills that delivers electricity to our homes? My own sense of wonder at quite simple artefacts was considerably increased after completing a workshop production course as part of my engineering training. The houses we live in, the machines with which we equip our homes, the cars we drive, are all the products of extraordinary design skills. This level of complexity can just seem to alienate us from the natural, God-given world. But it need not do. We could see in it the remarkable completion of God's creative activity and a source of abundant divine blessing.

Those purchases will be blessings that most truly reflect the co-creativity of God and humankind. (I am not quite so reticent as James Allcock in speaking about the human capacity to create things, or at least to complete the creative work that God has begun!) Christians should not be concerned just with price (although they will be to the extent that this reflects careful stewardship of resources) but also with quality, craftsmanship and art. My own church has just completed an extension to our church building. Of course price was important to us. But of equal importance has been the employment we have given to a local building firm, the whole congregation's shared concern for the design of the building, and the high aesthetic and functional quality of the result. I don't think anyone in our church would say we simply purchased extra space. The building is a blessing from God. It embodies our shared concern for extending God's work in our local area and reflects the creative skills of our architect and builders. It is easier to see this principle at work with church assets than with personal goods. But could we, indeed should we not, see the new car or video recorder in the same light? These are the products of the skill and labour of, albeit unseen, designers and production workers, through whom God blesses us and enables us to bring blessing to others.